Balloons

William K. Durr
Jean M. LePere
John J. Pikulski
Mary Lou Alsin

Consultant:
Hugh Schoephoerster

HOUGHTON MIFFLIN COMPANY   BOSTON

Atlanta   Dallas   Geneva, Illinois   Hopewell, New Jersey   Palo Alto   Toronto

Contents

Grateful acknowledgment is given for the contributions of Paul McKee.

Illustrators: pp. 3–12, JAMES MARSHALL; pp. 13, 20, 31, ELLEN APPLEBY; pp. 14–19, JANE DYER; pp. 21–30, DAVID McPHAIL; pp. 32–38, JAMES WATLING; p. 39, JILL WEBER; pp. 40–47, MARC BROWN.

Photographers: pp. 13, 20, 31, 39, Martucci Studio.

Book Cover by JÜRG FURRER. *Fabric design:* Copyright 1976 V.I.P., a Division of CRANSTON PRINT WORKS COMPANY.

Printed in the U.S.A.

ISBN: 0-395-31935-8

Bear and Frog

by JAMES MARSHALL

Frog: Surprise!
It is I.

Bear: Come in!
Come in, Frog.

Bear: Now I will get a surprise for you, Frog.

Frog: Can I help you, Bear?

Bear: You can help.

Frog: I like the surprise, Bear.

Bear: You like the surprise, Frog?
Now you will get a big surprise.

Bear: Come, Frog.

I want you to see the big surprise.

Frog: I want to see the big surprise.

Bear: You will like it.

Bear: Here is the big surprise.
Do you like it?

Frog: I like the surprise, Bear.

Bear: Come! We will get in, Frog.
We will go up.

Frog: I will get in.

I do not want to go up!

Bear: Come on, Frog.

You will like to go up.

You will see.

Bear: Up we go!

Frog: I do not like it in here.
I do not want to go up.
Help! Help!

Bear: Get up, Frog!

Here is a surprise you will like.

Come on! See the surprise.

Frog: I will not get up.

I want to go home!

Bear: Here it is, Frog.

Get up and see the surprise.

Do you like it here, Frog?

Frog: I like it here, Bear.

I can go home now.

Home is the best surprise!

Frog: I will go home, Bear.
I will jump in.

Bear: Jump in, Frog.
And I will go home.
Up, up, I go!

The Surprise Box

by TIM JOHNSON

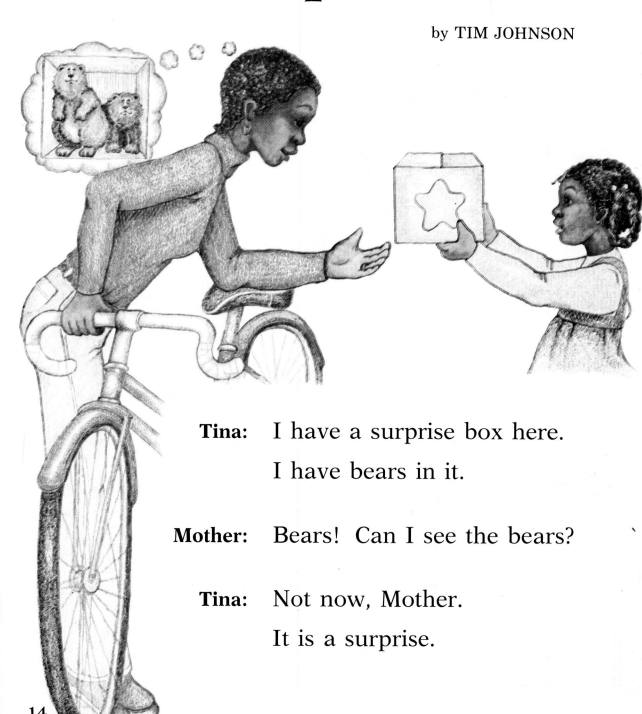

Tina: I have a surprise box here.
I have bears in it.

Mother: Bears! Can I see the bears?

Tina: Not now, Mother.
It is a surprise.

Father: What do you have in the box, Tina?

Tina: I have a fox, Father.

Father: Can I see the fox?

Tina: Not now, Father.
It is a surprise.
You will like it.

Andy: What do you have in the box, Tina?

Tina: I have pigs in here.

Andy: Pigs!

How can pigs get in a box?

Tina: You will see.

It is a good surprise.

You will like it.

Tina: I have a surprise box here.

I have a frog and a fish in it.

Mrs. Henry: How can a frog get in a box?

How can a fish get in a box?

Tina: You will see.

It's a good surprise.

Tina: Now come here!

Now you will see what is in the box.

You will get to see my surprises.

Mother: I want to see the bears.

Father: Now I will get to see the fox.

Andy: And I will see the pigs.

Mrs. Henry: Will I see a frog and a fish?

Tina: Surprise, surprise!

See my bears.

Here is my fox.

See my pigs.

Here is my frog.

And here is my fish.

Andy: Now we see!

You do have good surprises!

Have a Good Swim!

by DAVID McPHAIL

Bear: Get up, Frog!

Get up!

I want you to come for a swim.

Fox: Come on, Frog!

Bear wants you to come for a swim.

Bear: What do you see, Fox?

Is Frog home?

Fox: Frog is home.

Frog is not up.

Fox: We can't get Frog up.
What will we do?

Bear: We will get Frog up.

Fox: How will we get Frog up?

Bear: We can do it.
You will see.

Fox: What is in the box?

Why do you have it?

Bear: You will see.

You will see why I have this box.

Bear: Here, this is for you.

Fox: Why?

Bear: This will help you get Frog up.
This will do it.

Fox: Why do I have to get Frog up?
What will you do?

Bear: You will see.

Bear: Get up, Frog!

Get up and come for a swim!

Fox: Frog did not get up.

Can we go now?

I do want to go for a swim.

Bear: We can't go now.

I want Frog to come for a swim.

Frog likes to swim.

Fox: Now what do you have?

What is that for?

Bear: This will get Frog up.

We will get Frog to come for a swim.

Here, you can help me.

Fox: This will have to get Frog up.

It's the best we can do.

Bear: Come on, Frog!

Get up! Get up!

Get up and come for a swim.

Fox: Get up, Frog!

Get up and come for a swim!

Frog: Do you want to swim?

OK, Bear! OK, Fox!

I will help you swim.

Have a good swim!

Father can swim.   Holly can't swim.

Holly surprises Father.

A Fish for Sam

Sam: Will you take me to get a fish?
I want to take a fish to school.

Mother: Why do you want a fish?
You can't have a fish in school.

Sam: I can take a fish to school.
I can take it on Fish Day.

Father: Can you take this fish to school?

Sam: I do not want to take that fish.

Mother: You do not have to take that fish.
I will help you get a fish.
You will have it for Fish Day.

Bob: I have a fish for Fish Day.

Sam: I have a fish, too.

Bob: Is it a real fish, Sam?

Sam: You will see.
You will see my fish on Fish Day.

Sam: My fish is this big.
And it can fly!

Bob: How can a fish fly?
Fish can't fly, Sam.

Sam: My fish can fly!

Sam: This is the big day.
Is that your fish, Bob?

Bob: This is my fish.

Sam: I like your fish, Bob.

Jan: I do, too.
Here is my fish.
It's not a real fish.

Sam: That is a good fish, Jan.

Bob: We want to see your fish, Sam.

Sam: Here is my fish.
It can fly.

Jan: What is that, Sam?
That is not a fish.
How can that fly?

Sam: It can fly.
You will see.

THIS IS FISH DAY.

Jan: It is a fish!

Bob: And it can fly.
See it go!

Jan: That is a good fish, Sam.
We like your fish.

Kites

This kite is like a fish.

This big kite is like a fly.

This is a box kite.

Buzzy and the Pencil

by BONNIE BROWN WALMSLEY

Mindy: Come on, Buzzy.

This is a school day.

We have to go to school now.

Buzzy: I have to find my fox, Mindy.

I want to take it to school.

Buzzy: I can't find that fox.

Where is it?

Mindy   Did you look in this box?

Buzzy: I did.

It's not in that box.

Mindy: Buzzy, look here!

This looks like a fox.

Is this the fox you can't find?

Buzzy: That is my fox!

Mindy: Come on.

We have to go to school now.

Buzzy: Now I can't find my book.

I need that book for school.

Will you help me look for it?

Mindy: Buzzy, this looks like a school book.

Is this the book you need?

Buzzy: Good! That is the book I need.

Buzzy: Now I have my fox and my book.

Mindy: Good! Now we can go to school.

Buzzy: I have to take a pencil to school.
Where is my pencil?
I can't find it.

Mindy: We can go to school now, Buzzy.

You have your fox and your book.

And you have your pencil, too!

Buzzy: Do I have my pencil?

Where is it?

Mindy: Come and take a look, Buzzy.

You will see your pencil.

Buzzy: How do you like that!

Buzzy: Come on, Mindy!

We have to get to school now.

Sounds You Know

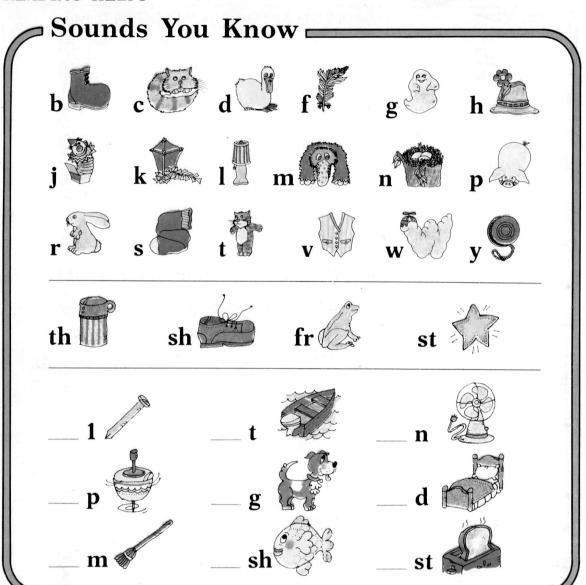

b   c   d   f   g   h

j   k   l   m   n   p

r   s   t   v   w   y

th   sh   fr   st

___ l   ___ t   ___ n

___ p   ___ g   ___ d

___ m   ___ sh   ___ st

New Sounds

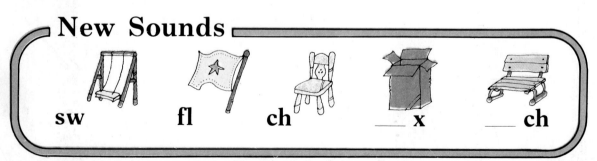

sw   fl   ch   ___ x   ___ ch